W9-BFM-102

Turning to God in Tough Times

Prayers to Comfort the Heart and Sustain the Spirit

Joan Guntzelman

theWORD
among us®
press

Published by The Word Among Us Press
7115 Guilford Road
Frederick, Maryland 21704
www.wau.org

15 14 13 12 11   1 2 3 4 5

ISBN: 978-1-59325-189-5
eISBN: 978-1-59325-416-2

Cover design by Faceout Studios.

Made and printed in the United States of America

Library of Congress Cataloging-in-Publication Data

Guntzelman, Joan, 1937-
  Turning to God in tough times : prayers to comfort the heart and sustain the spirit / Joan Guntzelman.
    p. cm.
  ISBN 978-1-59325-189-5
  1. Consolation--Meditations. 2. Suffering—Religious aspects—Christianity—Meditations. 3. Prayers—Christianity. 4. Devotional literature. I. Title. II. Title: Prayers to comfort the heart and sustain the spirit.
  BV4905.3.G86 2011
  242'.4--dc23
                                    2011023130

OTHER BOOKS BY JOAN GUNTZELMAN

God Knows You're Grieving:
Things to Do to Help You Through

Blessing Life's Losses

124 Prayers for Caregivers

Come, Healing God: Prayers During Illness

A Retreat with Mother Teresa and Damien of Molokai:
Caring for Those Who Suffer

Surrendering Our Stress: Prayers to Calm the Soul and
Strengthen the Spirit

For my brother Ray,
in gratitude for all his loving, skillful, patient, and
generous technical help, without which this book
would not have happened.

TABLE OF CONTENTS

INTRODUCTION

Through tears of frustration, helplessness, and great distress, a patient's husband cries out in a plaintive voice that reverberates off the hospital walls: "Why does it have to be so hard to be a human being?"

That question has been asked many times throughout the ages. We humans struggle with the vicissitudes of life on earth. So often our joys and delights are knocked aside by suffering and hardship. No matter how hard we try to avoid the painful aspects of life, they pop up when we least expect them. They challenge us as we try to cope with and conquer them. Sometimes our efforts are successful, and we find a way to ease, repair, or remove the hardships. At other times they claim the upper hand, and we struggle to find a way to live with them and to ameliorate their effects and the suffering and pain they bring to our lives.

Such suffering can emerge from physical, emotional, or interpersonal problems. There seems to be no end to their variety and composition. We all come up against hard times, even in our younger years. We search for ways to avoid problems, or we search for solutions or resolutions to keep them at bay. We often hold on to the fantasy that we could—or even should—go through life without them.

As we grow in wisdom, however, we realize that we will never be totally without hard times. Such experiences are simply part of being human. We would not know light without knowing darkness. Sometimes chaos threatens us, and then, before we know it, we find order and peace again. We grow and develop in the course of the cycles of life, through the many "little deaths" we endure and the "new life" that comes out of them. Eventually, we face diminishment and physical death, but always in the hope that we will experience everlasting life in Christ.

Each of our experiences gives us choices to make. While many of our struggles arise through no fault of our own, we also sometimes bring about our own distress and trouble by what we say or do. We need to be aware of those instances when we create or contribute to the suffering we experience. We also need to know that in the challenges we face are hidden gifts that we can look for and find if we choose to do so.

Above all, we must always remember that God is holding us and carrying us close to his heart, sustaining our every breath. Without that support, we would not exist. Deep down, we know that God lives and loves us. It is that awareness that sends us to God in our distress. We somehow know that the help we can find to support us through our struggles comes from our God.

Yet sometimes when we are going through tough times, we find it difficult to pray. My hope is that the one hundred reflections in this book will help those who are struggling to connect with God. Each reflection begins with a verse or two from the Scriptures, moves into a short meditation, and ends with a prayer. The prayer is meant to launch readers into their own conversation with the Lord. Through our decision to quiet ourselves and come into the presence of God, we can find the strength and courage we need to endure our trials. The Lord will truly comfort our hearts and sustain our spirits. He is our refuge in times of trouble, and he will not abandon us!

Joan Guntzelman

God's Radiance

[May] the LORD make his face to shine upon you,
and be gracious to you.

—NUMBERS 6:25

When times are tough and when our path is dark and unclear, we forget that God is still close to us. None of our hard and painful times can chase God away. In fact, more than ever, this is when God is very near to us. We just need to ask him to shine his face upon us and on all who are experiencing hard times. God's radiance will warm us, and we will feel his love and care. Then the peace that only God can give will replace the great distress we feel.

Great God of peace, who loves all that you have made, I come to you and ask your blessing on me and on all who are suffering. May the radiance of your face, the sign of your love, permeate me. I trust that you have a lesson for me in this difficult situation. If I've contributed to these trials in any way, show me how. Give me the wisdom to find my way through them. And then, my dear God, help me find peace.

Pursuing the Lord

The LORD is good to those who look to him,
to anyone who seeks him.

—LAMENTATIONS 3:25 (REB)

We seek many things in life—happiness, fun, health, good relationships, money. We may even judge our success by the amount of things we accrue, and often we cannot get enough of them. What might our lives be like if we actively pursued God, if we made that a conscious endeavor? As we journey through the ups and downs that are part of life, how different would we be if we sought God? What would our troubles and our delights be like if we purposefully sought God in them?

Creator God, what would my life look like if I chose to actively seek you? I know I could expect to share in the same experiences as others—all the joys as well as all the struggles, illnesses, and losses—but I would do it all with more of an awareness of your presence. Just as I put effort into looking for other things, help me to consciously look for you in all the circumstances of my life. When I find myself in a difficult place, I might say, "God, help me to find you here. Help me to see you in my struggles, in the person who is upset with me or dislikes me, and in all of my hard times." May I also find you in everything delightful and enjoyable.

ALL THINGS ARE PASSING

See, the former things have come to pass,
and new things I now declare.

—ISAIAH 42:9

Nothing stays the same. The pattern of the universe is one of dying and rising, coming to be and passing away. Sometimes the passing is easy and pleasant, and sometimes it carries great pain and distress as life asks us to let go and move on. Many of the times we find the most difficult come about as we wrench ourselves away from a prior stage of growth or a connection to loved ones.

How quickly my life is moving, loving God! I've been blessed with so many gifts and opportunities, yet my most painful times have been when it was time to let go of any of those gifts. It's so hard. I realize that change is just the way life is, but I really struggle with losing what is precious to me. Help me to remember that you are with me through every stage of my life. Help me to get through my hard times so that I can move forward to receive the new blessings you want to pour out on me.

LIGHT MY PATH WITH YOUR WORD

Your word is a lamp to my feet
and a light to my path.

—PSALM 119:105

When our lives are in trouble, we search for something or someone to guide us. If God's word lights our paths and leads us in the way we should go, then perhaps we should make it a practice to spend even a short time each day reading the holy Scriptures. We might read a favorite passage or even choose a selection at random, asking God for its gifts. We might be surprised and delighted at how pertinent we find the passage we've chosen.

I will read a short passage and then ponder it for a bit, sitting quietly. I can ask, "Holy Spirit, what do you want me to learn in these words? What is your wisdom for me here?" Then as I move on to my daily activities, I will allow these words to stay with me, and I will remain open to any new thoughts that arise. Holy Spirit, bring to my mind anything that will help me as I go about my day.

BREAKING FREE

So they cried to the LORD in their trouble,
and he saved them from their distress;
he brought them out of the dark, the deepest darkness,
and burst their chains.

—PSALM 107:13-14 (REB)

Often we get ourselves all tangled up in our worries and distress. Then our anxiety and fears become like chains that bind us and keep us from moving forward. How can we break free when we become only more and more enmeshed in our emotions? Our chains may be broken only when we decide that it's time to ask for help. When we see that we're not making much progress on our own and we cry out to the Lord in our trouble, help comes.

Here I am, Lord, in a place of "deepest darkness," and I can't find my way out. I don't seem to be able to undo my chains by myself, as hard as I try. Help me understand what I need to learn from this terrible time, and please show me how to keep myself free. I count on you!

Hope Does Not Disappoint

We boast in our hope of sharing the glory of God. . . .
And hope does not disappoint us.

—Romans 5:2, 5

In the midst of our difficulties and struggles, we worry about what we'll have to contend with, and we're tempted to give up. Our tendency is to abandon real hope and settle into "wishes" that are casual and fleeting. But our true hope is in Christ. We must hold on to Jesus and his promises with rock-solid certainty that we will someday share in his glory. He will not disappoint us!

Great God of power and might, I love you and I hope in you with all my heart. I know that you would never have promised us anything in which we couldn't have absolute trust. Strengthen my belief and trust in you and my solid conviction that not the tiniest drop of my hope in you is in vain. You are my rock, my stronghold, my deliverer, and my love.

Return to Your God

But as for you, return to your God,
hold fast to love and justice,
and wait continually for your God.

—Hosea 12:6

When times are difficult, it's easy to get lost in worry and fear and even to sink into despair. When we are in such a state, we often distract ourselves with things, events, and diversions that take us into unhealthy and unhelpful directions. We drift further and further from God in both our thoughts and actions. And without prayer and the sacraments, we have no foundation to support us.

Bring me back to you, God of love and justice. Hold me close to you so that I won't be lost. You are my foundation, so essential to every breath I take. How could I ever live without you as the central focus of my life? Come to me without delay. I need you, and so I will wait continually for you.

CHRIST IN YOU

*To them God chose to make known how great among
the Gentiles are the riches of the glory of this mystery,
which is Christ in you, the hope of glory.*

—COLOSSIANS 1:27

Too often we imagine God as somehow hovering in some distant "heaven" far, far away. Especially when times are challenging and threaten us, we need to remember that each of us is carrying Christ in us. Jesus is alive and at work in us and in this world of ours. He is the breath of our breath, the love in our hearts, and he is delighted when we give him an opportunity to be at work in the world. Perhaps our first waking moment could be an acknowledgement of that truth and all that it means for us: Jesus lives in us and wants us to be his hope for the world.

Good morning, Jesus living in me! Thank you for being with me through the night and now for being here to use me in your work today. I am grateful for the opportunities you give me. Direct me and guide me today, through good and beautiful times and through my struggles. I delight in being the place where you choose to dwell. Keep me aware of that great privilege, and help me to see you in all whom I encounter today.

Jesus' Healing Touch

"Lord, I am not worthy to have you come under my roof; but only speak the word, and my servant will be healed."

—Matthew 8:8

How often do we need healing in our lives! At times we long for a physical healing, and at other times, we are most in need of an emotional healing. Sometimes we need both. During his time on earth, Jesus performed many miraculous healings. Do we believe that the Lord can heal us, even today? We shouldn't be afraid to ask. The Roman centurion believed that Jesus could heal his servant just through his word, and so it happened. Jesus praised this man for his great faith (Matthew 8:10). So go ahead and step out in faith. We may not get the exact healing we are looking for, but God always heals us in some way when we come to him with expectant faith.

Jesus, I am hurting and in need of your healing touch. I know that through your word, you have the power to heal me. Give me the faith of the centurion so that I may come to you in faith and know that you will listen to my prayer. Lord, I also want to be a source of healing for others. Show me how to be a soothing balm to those who are hurting.

GIVING THANKS FOR THE BODY

*I do not cease to give thanks for you as I
remember you in my prayers.*

—EPHESIANS 1:16

As we look back over the difficult times in our lives, we often discover that we came through the difficulties because of the presence of certain people. These were people who not only loved and cared for us but who also showed us, without speaking, how present God was in their own lives. We knew that God was the central focus of their lives, and we saw God at work through the love they showed to us. How blessed we've been to have such brothers and sisters in Christ!

My gratitude for all of those who've helped me through the years is overflowing! I find it impossible to remember each and every person who has nourished and guided me through the hard times in my life. But God, you know who they are! Please shower them all with your wonderful blessings. Let me bless them by learning how to be present to those in my life who need my help and support.

Choose to Bring a Blessing

Bless those who persecute you; bless and do not curse them.

—Romans 12:14

When we're in conflict with others or see them as the source of our distress, our inclination is to send back to them what has been so hard for us to take. Hence, we begin a cycle of anger and revenge, attack and blame. Love is absent, along with peace, only to be replaced by bitterness and resentment. St. Paul apparently recognized that someone needs be strong enough to break that cycle. Instead of cursing the other person, we need to bring genuine love and blessing into the situation.

As I look at this behavior, God of peace and love, I realize how easy it is for me to keep the conflict going. I don't want to be the one contributing to the situation. I do want to be one who brings a blessing. But I have to choose to make this happen. Only I can decide; then I have to do it. Help me to bring peace and blessing to every area of my life and to everyone with whom I come in contact.

God Is at Work

"Take heart, it is I; do not be afraid."

—Matthew 14:27

Are we willing to accept that God can be present and at work in all kinds of situations? Would it change our way of dealing with problems if we said to ourselves, "God is at work here"? Or maybe we could ask ourselves, "What might God want me to learn or gain from this problem?" God is in our troubles as well as in our joys. This truth can help us to "take heart" and "not be afraid."

Help me to get past my fear, O Lord. When times are tough, I know that you are with me and that you work in every situation, even the hard ones, to draw me closer to you. I don't want to be overcome by fear and anxiety. I choose to take heart! I give you my fear, and I ask you to support me and hold me up.

Listen and Pay Attention

If you love to listen you will gain knowledge,
and if you pay attention you will become wise.

—Sirach 6:33

Sometimes problems need to be addressed with new wisdom. Finding new wisdom, however, requires that we be open to new sources—ones that we may not have been aware of or that we were closed off to previously. If we show a willingness to listen and pay attention, we may discover a better solution to our problems. We may also be able to better discern what can help or hurt us. And when we address our problems creatively, we may also find our own wisdom expanding. With our newfound wisdom, we may even become a good resource for others.

Gracious God, help me recognize that I don't know it all. I want to be open to learning new things. Remind me how important it is to choose well what I give my attention to. Support me in growing in wisdom by making me aware of the wisdom that is available around me. And with any wisdom I gain, may it contribute to the resolution not only of my own problems but of others as well.

God Knows Us Completely

O Lord, you have searched me and known me.
You know when I sit down and when I rise up;
you discern my thoughts from far away.
You search out my path and my lying down,
and are acquainted with all my ways.
Even before a word is on my tongue,
O Lord, you know it completely.

—Psalm 139:1-4

How amazing, O Creator God, that you know us through and through! We can't hide anything from you—you know everything about us. When we're sad, terrified, or feeling helpless or guilty, you are right here with us. When we're flourishing and feeling joyful, content, and grateful, there you are also. So both in our good and bad times, encourage us to remember your loving presence and turn to you with confidence and hope. You know us better than we know ourselves. May we look to you to understand who we are and what we need.

Loving God, it's so good for me to remind myself that you were aware of my distress even before I was. I want to be sure now that I also come to you when things are going well in my life. You also know what delights me even before I do, and yet you still are grateful for my remembering you and your presence. And because you know me so well, please help me to understand myself and who you intend me to be.

Look to the Light

"I am the light of the world."

—John 8:12

As children, most of us just "knew" that there were monsters hiding under our beds or in our closets or behind the trees and bushes in our yards. Darkness has always been the place where scary creatures live—both real and imaginary. And no matter how "big" we get, we often find that some of those scary creatures have come along with us, perhaps in a different form than when we were children. It still helps to have someone bigger and stronger than we are to hold onto when we encounter those times in our lives when we're afraid. When we decide to take hold of Jesus, we will find the guidance and strength to carry us through to the light.

My loving Jesus, light of the world, you have conquered the darkness. You are with me in all of my times of darkness and shadow, holding some gift or some wisdom for me to find there. I may be amazed at finding wisdom in such unexpected places, but if you are there, so is your wisdom. Help me always to look for it. You alone are able to recognize my fears and keep the "scary creatures" in my life at bay.

FINDING GOD IN THE PRESENT

"Sleeper, awake!
Rise from the dead,
and Christ will shine on you."

—EPHESIANS 5:14

Many times we walk around as if we are asleep—neither awake nor aware. Yet in our everyday lives, we are surrounded by miracles. When we get caught up fretting about all our worries and problems, however, we miss the gift of the present moment. We don't realize that we never have the past or the future but only the present. May we wake up from the darkness of our unawareness and come into the brightness of this moment, which is the only place where God is waiting for us.

Shine your light on me, dear Jesus. I fall "asleep" because I am focused only on my troubles and fail to see the miracles in my life. Wake me up, and let me walk every single moment of my day with an awareness that your face is shining on me and that you are with me, even when the walking is tough. Let me see that every moment is holy and contributes to my journey of becoming who you want me to be.

Prepare Yourself for Testing

My child, when you come to serve the Lord,
prepare yourself for testing.

—Sirach 2:1

Almost everything we do in life requires some training and preparation. The more important the job and the more it will affect us and others, the more necessary is our willingness to learn and be tested. Each of us provides God with a place to manifest himself in this world, to work through our very being. What a huge responsibility for us! Surely we can expect to be tested as we present ourselves to God for such important service. But what an amazing privilege to be used in this way!

With all my heart, I thank you for letting me serve you in such a way, my dear God. As I walk through this world, I want to remember that you use my hands, my feet, and my heart to touch other people. As someone once said, "You have to allow God to wear your face." How blessed I am when you give me opportunities to be your face in the world. When you test me even in hard times, may you always find me doing well in your service.

Defend Me, O Lord!

My eyes are turned towards you, O GOD, my Lord;
in you I seek refuge; do not leave me defenseless.

—PSALM 141:8

Sometimes we look for help and the resolution of our problems in places that can't help us or may even make our situation worse. How important for us to be honest with ourselves and choose our support in healthy, life-giving ways. We need to be sure that any help we seek comes from trustworthy sources. We can rely on God to protect us when we ask ourselves, "Is this a godly way to deal with the situation?" With the Lord as our refuge, we will not go astray.

My loving God, I count on you to be my defense whenever I'm in the midst of troubles and hard times. Please don't let me get caught up in things that make the situation worse. Be my refuge, and let me hold tightly to your protection. I trust in you.

Be Merciful

"Be merciful, just as your Father is merciful. Do not judge, and you will not be judged; do not condemn, and you will not be condemned. Forgive, and you will be forgiven; give, and it will be given to you. A good measure, pressed down, shaken together, running over, will be put into your lap; for the measure you give will be the measure you get back."

—Luke 6:36-38

Disagreements and difficulties among people can sometimes seem to go on forever. When we refuse to see the other side, to listen, or to offer peace or goodwill, or when we are unwilling to talk or work things out, we tend to prolong our distress. Yet when we pray, "Forgive us our sins as we forgive those who sin against us," we lock ourselves into a potentially frightening contract: If we aren't forgiving, then we may not be forgiven. That can have tragic implications for all involved. Where, then, is our mercy?

Forgiving God, I know that so many of my difficulties come about through arguments and disagreements. When I refuse to reconsider, to talk something out, or to forgive, I keep the problems alive. Please soften my spirit, and help me to be open to working through things. I've seen families torn apart for a lifetime because of their unwillingness to forgive. Help me to be merciful with others and with myself. Strengthen me in my ability to forgive. When I want to forgive and can't do it on my own, give me your grace to do it.

Do Everything in Love

Keep alert, stand firm in your faith, be courageous, be strong. Let all that you do be done in love.

—1 Corinthians 16:13-14

St. Paul gives us clear instructions on how to act when we feel anxious or fearful or when we are threatened with danger. In our struggles, we can choose the "weapons" we will use to respond. We don't have to fight with the same destructive techniques that our adversaries use or that the world tells us are the most effective. Instead, we can choose faith, courage, strength, and the most powerful weapon of all: love. When all our behavior is grounded in love, we will be victorious, no matter what the outcome!

God of power and might, help me always be aware that no one decides my behavior but me. Whatever happens to me, I can choose to build up or destroy. When the battles are over, I want to look back and be at peace with the ways in which I chose to respond. Let me always choose love.

The Treasure That Lies Hidden

I will give you the treasures of darkness
and riches hidden in secret places.

—Isaiah 45:3

We tend to think of darkness as being negative and undesirable, something to be avoided. So what could the "treasures" and "riches" of the darkness be? Could it be that the difficulties of life that challenge us and pull us into dark places are the fertile soil for our growth in the Lord? Perhaps darkness prevents our being distracted from what's important in life, such as our relationship with God. Perhaps the light shines more brightly when we've been tested by times of darkness.

God, help me come to see that it's you who is hidden and waiting in all of my dark times. Perhaps you are the treasure and riches I find when I give myself to the darkness and am open to finding its gifts. May I always be on the lookout for you, even in the unlikeliest places in which you choose to wait for me.

FROM THE DEPTHS GOD HEARS US

I called on your name, O LORD,
from the depths of the pit;
you heard my plea, "Do not close your ear
to my cry for help, but give me relief!"
You came near when I called on you;
you said, "Do not fear!"

—LAMENTATIONS 3:55-57

We eventually make our way through most of our traumas and difficulties. It may take a lot of prayer, struggle, hard work, and help from others, but we get there. Sometimes, however, we feel unable to move forward. We find life excruciating and painful, and we feel overwhelmed, exhausted, and depressed. From the depths of this "pit," as the prophet Jeremiah says in the Book of Lamentations, we must turn to God. As we cry out for help, God will come near and say to us, "Do not fear!"

Come to my help, dear God of my salvation. Hear me! Help me! I am in great distress and I can't do this alone. There is no way I can do anything without you. Reach out your arms and your heart to me and bring me relief and comfort. Hold me close to you and let me feel the warmth of your love and presence.

What Really Matters

And this is my prayer, that your love may grow ever richer in knowledge and insight of every kind, enabling you to learn by experience what things really matter.

—Philippians 1:9-10 (REB)

Most of our lives are filled up with "things." We spend our time and energy buying, saving, and searching for things that we hope will make us happy. Yet St. Paul suggests that if our love grows, we'll begin to understand what really matters. The things we collect or crave—whether they are material things, experiences, titles, or power—won't make us happy for long. Our true "riches" can be found only in God and his love for us.

Help me begin to sort through and unclutter my life, my God, clearing out things that in the long run aren't important. Perhaps this is a good time to focus more on the wisdom and love you bring to my life, from which will come my growth in understanding and insight. Be with me as I think about these things. Be with me as I clarify my values so that I come to see what really matters. Make my prayer grow "ever richer in knowledge and insight."

Recognizing Our Need

On the day I called, you answered me,
you increased my strength of soul.

—Psalm 138:3

When we never acknowledge that we have a need, we run the risk of never having our need met. Though we may receive many gifts without asking for them, in some cases we must recognize our neediness and then ask for help. When we go to God and ask him to help us, he may answer us directly, or he may lead us to ask for that help from people we know. Unless we reach out for these blessings and do what it takes to receive them, we may never find them. Only our willingness to ask opens the lock in the door.

Jesus, you told us to ask if we wanted to receive. You hold so many treasures for us. If our hearts are open and we ask you for these blessings, you give them to us. Help me to be aware of all the blessings you have in store for me. I want my wholeness and strength to come from you. I'll begin now by thanking you for all that you have given me, and I will also ask you to open my eyes to all that you have in store for me—if I but only ask.

GOD'S COMPASSION

For a brief moment I abandoned you,
but with great compassion I will gather you.
In overflowing wrath for a moment
I hid my face from you,
but with everlasting love I will have compassion on you,
says the LORD, your Redeemer.

—ISAIAH 54:7-8

How many times do we feel like we've been abandoned? When darkness and heaviness press us down, we feel frightened and helpless, and we believe that we have nowhere to turn. Yet we know that God will never abandon us, even for a second. Perhaps this Scripture passage can help us. How reassuring to know that even if God's face is hidden from us right at this moment, he is still here with us. Perhaps just the image of God's compassionate face drawing us back to his everlasting love will speak to us and reassure us that he will never forsake us.

Your compassion, my God, means that you are suffering with me, that you are feeling my pain and the fear that I've lost you. I sit here very close to you and I reach out for your embrace. You are the God who said that you would never forget me. Hold me close in the radiance of your presence, and take away my fears. Shine your face on me so brightly that I am never tempted to feel that you've abandoned me.

The Gift of Unity

*How very good and pleasant it is
when kindred live together in unity!*

—Psalm 133:1

Living together peaceably doesn't necessarily happen without effort. Choices and decisions for living well together need to be consciously and purposefully made. We must choose to honor and respect one another and to readily forgive when we are offended. We must choose love and kindness over sarcasm and anger. How many families would be healthier and happier if they abided by such precepts? And when we live in such a supportive environment, how much easier it is to cope with the hard times that may come. Today I might ask myself, "How can I create an environment that is a good and pleasant place to be?"

Help me today, loving God of peace, to choose to live
well with those in my world. Let me contribute to
unity, and when I have a disagreement, help me to
work it out for the good of the group. I choose not to
contribute to dissensions and destructive comments
that tear down our unity and destroy our relationships.

Reaching for the Stars

Do all things without murmuring and arguing,
so that you may be blameless and innocent, children of God
without blemish in the midst of a crooked and perverse
generation, in which you shine like stars in the world.

—Philippians 2:14-15

How many choices we are faced with every day of our lives! Here St. Paul asks us whether we want to contribute to the perversity of the world or choose to "shine like stars." We know what it's like to be in the midst of grumbling and arguing, and how our words can build up or tear down. By our choices we contribute to one or the other. May we always reach for the stars in what we offer to others and to the world.

I'm so aware, my God, of how negativity and destructive comments can affect my loved ones and those with whom I interact. I want to create a loving atmosphere, not one filled with strife and resentment. I know there are times to be constructively critical, but please help me to be life-giving in my comments. I want to be a star that shines for you!

Stepping Out of Ignorance

"I have come as light into the world, so that everyone who believes in me should not remain in the darkness."

—John 12:46

What could be the darkness in which we remain? Darkness is often likened to ignorance, and sometimes we can willfully choose to be in a state of unknowing. For example, we might refuse to learn or we might refuse to acknowledge what we know to be true. We might recognize what the wisdom of God is asking of us and also choose to ignore it. If we think that remaining in darkness releases us from responsibility, we might refuse to step up and take action when it's called for.

St. Peter, you remained in darkness when you refused to acknowledge that you knew Jesus. Come to my assistance! I don't want to remain in darkness. Pray that I will have the courage to step out of my hiding places and own up to what I know is the truth. May the darkness not shield me from whatever I need to do.

GOD NEVER TURNS AWAY FROM US

For as the heavens are higher than the earth,
so are my ways higher than your ways
and my thoughts than your thoughts.

—ISAIAH 55:9

One thing we must surely believe is that God's ears will never be closed to our cries for help. We must remind ourselves of that truth and rest in that knowledge. Even though we can turn our attention away from someone in need, God is always aware of our distress and our cries for help and never turns away from us. However, God's response may not be what we want or expect. Those may be the times, then, when we challenge ourselves to remember that God's ways are not our ways. He always has the whole picture in mind and will respond to our call with his perfect timing.

I thank you for hearing me, my loving God, and for being here with me in my fears and worries. Help me to be strong in my faith in you. As I release all my fears to you, I will continue to remind myself that you are with me in all of my worries, and that I can trust in you.

A Place to Pray

"Sit here while I go over there and pray."
—MATTHEW 26:36

How many times in the Scriptures do we hear of Jesus going off to pray? The primary message seems to be the importance of praying—of raising one's heart, mind, and spirit to God. Praying was a way for Jesus to momentarily retreat from the situation at hand and ground himself in his heavenly Father's love, especially when he was weary or facing something very difficult and challenging. He often chose places in the natural world—mountains, hillsides, seashores, and then the garden of Gethsemane as he prepared for his final suffering and death. Do we also find opportunities to back off from the harshness of the moment and search for clarity and strength in God?

Remind me, Jesus, when I'm about to embark on something difficult or when I just need a break, that you are close. So that I can do this well, I choose a place that is conducive to prayer, knowing that you will be there with me. When I use this particular place often to pray, I know that just my coming to this spot may trigger my peacefulness and my prayer. And this is my prayer: that your love may overflow more and more in me, giving me the strength and wisdom that I need.

GOD WILL PROVIDE A WAY OUT

God is faithful, and he will not let you be tested beyond your strength, but with the testing he will also provide the way out so that you may be able to endure it.

—1 CORINTHIANS 10:13

At every stage of our lives, we are faced with times of testing that challenge us and give us choices to make and directions to choose. Through difficult times or when we are unsure of what to do, God walks with us, supporting us and encouraging us to make the right choices. How important it is for us to trust God in such times of testing! God will give us a "way out" of our troubles and will not test us beyond our strength.

In the journey of my life, Lord, I count on you to steer me in the direction that leads to my becoming all that you want me to be. I can remind myself that you know exactly what I'm going through and that you won't desert me, even if I stumble along. Let me see the hard times now as stepping stones to wholeness. Hold my hand to keep me steady as I step out. I know that you will provide me with a way out of my troubles.

All Things Work for Good

We know that all things work together for good for those who love God, who are called according to his purpose.

—Romans 8:28

When we find ourselves in the depths of distress or worry and don't know what to do or what is to become of us, it can be so important to remind ourselves that we don't have the last word. We aren't the ones in charge. If we love God and trust in the certainty that St. Paul expresses, we can count on the ultimate good to emerge. There is no discrimination here: All things work together for good.

I love you, my God, and I know that you love me and have called me into being. May all your purposes for me and my life come to fruition. Increase my trust in you, and let me never doubt that you and your love will emerge in all of the situations in which I find myself. I know that the ultimate good will be living with you eternally in heaven.

God Hears Us

And this is the boldness we have in him, that if we
ask anything according to his will, he hears us.

—1 John 5:14

When our days are painful or difficult and nothing seems to change, and when we pray for help but find only darkness and frustration, we are inclined to assume that our prayers aren't "getting through" to God. This is the time to examine our thinking. The Scriptures clearly say that God hears us when we pray. Perhaps we need to remind ourselves that God may be answering our requests in ways that emerge from his wisdom—ways that we may not see or understand at the time.

God of wisdom, I know that you don't suffer with "selective inattention" like I do. You hear all of my requests; you do not miss even a word of what I think or say. Strengthen my boldness and trust in you. Let me never stop asking for what I need. I believe that you hear me each time I ask, but you know my needs better than I do. So remind me not to doubt: All I have to do is make my request to you, and you will hear me. Then I can count on your attention, trusting that you will allow what you believe to be best for me.

The Kingdom of God Is Near

From that time Jesus began to proclaim,
"Repent, for the kingdom of heaven has come near."

—Matthew 4:17

"Repent" is another way of saying, "Look again! Look freshly!"
or of saying, "Come to this with a new mind." With this approach,
we might hear Jesus saying to us, "You think the kingdom of
heaven is far off, but it's really quite close to you!" When times
are tough and we worry over what's happening or where we're
going, perhaps the most important thing we can do is "repent."
We need to look beyond ourselves to see how we're meant to help
bring about the kingdom of God on earth—not just for ourselves,
but for those around us as well.

Jesus, help me to see and believe that your kingdom
is not far off somewhere but right here in the people,
situations, and places I encounter every day. I want
to work with you to make the kingdom come alive
today. Show me opportunities to make you known
to others. I want to live in your kingdom all the days
of my life!

God Will Not Fail You

"It is the LORD who goes before you. He will be with you; he will not fail you or forsake you. Do not fear or be dismayed."

—DEUTERONOMY 31:8

Life can lead us in a million directions. Often we don't even know where we're going until we get there! How important it is for us to always be aware of just who is leading us. In all of our endeavors, it's far too easy to be "carried along by the 'nobody' without making any real choices," as the philosopher Martin Heidegger once said. May we be clear about who we choose to put at the front of our line—the God who will not fail us.

The longer I live in this world of countless lifestyles and choices—all of which can be either life-giving or death-dealing—the more clearly I need to be aware of what I choose and who I choose to lead me. I choose you, my God, who will not fail me. I choose you, the One who always encourages me to follow you. Without doubt, you will not fail me nor forsake me.

God's Plan for Our Lives

Surely I know the plans I have for you, says the LORD, plans for
your welfare and not for harm, to give you a future with hope.
Then when you call upon me and come and pray to me, I will hear
you. When you search for me, you will find me; if you seek me with
all your heart, I will let you find me, says the LORD.

—JEREMIAH 29:11-14

God has a wonderful plan for our lives. He wants to bless us, but
we have to show our intention and goodwill by taking our relationship with him seriously. Do we acknowledge him and ask him
for his grace? Do we raise our voices in prayer and ask him for
what we need? Our Lord wants us to put our whole heart into
searching for him and his blessings. If we don't, we may never
find what we're looking for.

Dear God, I'm so worried about my future. I need
you to enter into the troubles I'm in and help me find
my way through them. I need you and your grace in
my life. Hear me when I call upon you. Show me
what I need to do to improve my situation. I ask this
with all my heart. And I ask this, not only for me and
my own welfare, but also for all of my brothers and
sisters in this world who are also struggling and in
dire conditions.

Being Careful with Our Speech

"Listen and understand: it is not what goes into the mouth that
defiles a person, but it is what comes out of the mouth that defiles."
—Matthew 15:10-11

We can have a profound effect on one another for good or for ill, but we often remain unaware of our influence. One important way that we contribute to the growth or diminishment of others is by what we say. Our words can spark a wonderful movement toward making the world a better place, but they can also tear down and destroy. What a responsibility we have to be a force for good in the lives of others!

Holy Spirit of wisdom, truth, and love, let me always think twice before I speak. I want to contribute to the building up of this world rather than to its destruction, so let me choose my words thoughtfully and carefully. May I never defile your creation by choosing to use negative, critical, or malignant speech. Help me especially today to find opportunities to be positive, encouraging, and kind to others by what I say to them.

Rejoice in This Day

This is the day that the LORD has made;
let us rejoice and be glad in it.

—PSALM 118:24

Some days it feels like everything is going wrong. The stock market tumbles, it is raining heavily, we trip and fall, our car breaks down, or someone cuts in front of us in line. We glance in a mirror and think we're looking at someone much older or realize we've gained ten pounds. We wish we'd never gotten up that morning, and we spend the day grumbling and distressed. These are the times that challenge us to find God in our midst. Every day we wake up to is the day that the Lord has made, and that day will never come again. So perhaps we can acknowledge that fact and find a way to rejoice in the day—a gift that God has given us.

Thank you, my God, for the variety of experiences that I have in each day of each week. Each moment is new, and each event puts me to the test to see if I can find you there. Open my eyes to all the ways in which you may be touching me this day, even in the challenges. Let me find you in all your disguises.

ENLIGHTEN THE EYES OF OUR HEART

With the eyes of your heart enlightened, may [you] know
what is the hope to which he has called you.

—EPHESIANS 1:18

Rarely do we see reality for what it is. We get caught up in our own perceptions and fail to see that what we are missing or how the situation can be perceived in a different way. When times are difficult, we tend to exaggerate our problems and forget our blessings. Perhaps we are even tempted to despair. These are the times when we need to ask God to give light to the "eyes of our heart." God can show us how to see with his eyes—and that will give us a reason for hope!

Dear God, you are my life and my hope, both now and forever. You never give up on me. Lead me away from despair. Enlighten the eyes of my heart to see the truth of you everywhere. Help me to perceive reality as it is, not as I see it. Then I will have a hope that never fades.

UNBIND ME!

Jesus said to them, "Unbind him, and let him go."

—JOHN 11:44

Most of us think of ourselves as free and independent, living our lives as we choose. Yet these words of Jesus at the death of Lazarus could easily apply to all of us. How important it is to open our eyes to all that tethers us as we go about our lives. Often our attitudes, our ideas, our prejudices, or our habits and ways of living have trapped us and kept us bound. We hear ourselves saying, "This is just the way I am" or "This is how I've always done this," not realizing that we've developed "tombs" for ourselves that limit us. The story of Lazarus is clearly a war between death and life. Jesus and Lazarus both chose life.

Jesus, wherever I've chosen to tie myself up, wherever I've refused to grow, come to that place in me. Just as you did for Lazarus, untie the bonds that bury me or hold me back. When I don't even know what might be binding me up, show me where I'm trapped, and free me. In all my decisions, help me to choose life. I want to be free and grow in you. Move me out of the "tombs" that imprison me.

God Will Protect Us

He will hide me in his shelter
in the day of trouble;
he will conceal me under the cover of his tent;
he will set me high on a rock.

—Psalm 27:5

How important and touching it is to note the lengths to which our God will go to protect and help us in our troubles. Maybe we haven't realized that his "shelter" or "tent" can take on a variety of forms that are already at work in our lives to support us in our distress. Can we imagine what might serve as the "rock" he shares with us that removes us from the difficulties? Whatever the mode, what we do know is that God is working with us to deal with the troubles we face. We can count on it.

As I sit in my times of prayer, my God, I can bring myself to peace by closing my eyes and imagining you sitting with me in your place of shelter. I see all around us the brightness of your light that warms and strengthens me as I sit close to you. Assure me that you will always be with me. Bring me back to this place of light and love whenever I feel afraid. Please show me the "rock" that I am missing, that may help me out of my difficulties.

Mourning with Those Who Mourn

Do not avoid those who weep,
but mourn with those who mourn.

—Sirach 7:34

Throughout our lives we experience numerous losses and difficulties that bring us to tears. Some of our darkest hours and most painful times come with the loss of someone or something significant. We can lose the connections we've made with others, the expectation that life will remain as it is, or the image that we have of ourselves. Any of these losses can make us lose our bearings. Mourning and tears are normal expressions of human grief and necessary steps in moving forward and adjusting to the new reality we find ourselves in. When we mourn with others or when they mourn with us, we help one another in making our way through the darkness of grief.

Jesus, when your friend Lazarus died, you too joined the other mourners and wept at his tomb. Your willingness to join in their grief showed them how great was your love for the friend you held in common. Help me understand that when I share my own grief with others, we support each other in moving through our loss and sadness into new life.

Learning from Jesus

"Follow me."

—John 21:19

What is our path? What are we meant to "do" with our lives? How are we to live? What is God's plan for us? How do we know what direction to take when things are hard and we can't find the way? Is there anything or anyone we can rely on? We sometimes forget that we have someone who doesn't just tell us but shows us how to live. Countless events in our lives have a great similarity to Jesus' own experiences on this earth—praying, sharing friendships, learning from each other, challenging the authorities, and working together. He is the powerful One on whom we should pattern our lives.

Sit with me, Jesus, in my hard times, and let me talk with you and learn how I can "follow" you. You showed us a better way to live. You showed us how to love and care for one another. You were always honest. You called people to their higher and holier selves. You didn't use force or violence. So now, when I'm not sure which way to go, I can sit with my problem and figure out from what I know about your life just what you might want me to do. I want to pattern my life after you. Who else could I follow but you, my Lord and Savior?

God's Glory Is Upon You

Arise, shine; for your light has come,
and the glory of the LORD has risen upon you.
For darkness shall cover the earth,
and thick darkness the peoples;
but the LORD will arise upon you,
and his glory will appear over you.

—ISAIAH 60:1-2

How rarely do we give any thought at all to the fact that the glory of the Lord has risen upon us? We're quick to name our faults and failings, and we tend to focus on the "thick darkness" in our lives and in ourselves. But what about accepting and reminding ourselves that God's glory appears in us and through us? Perhaps we need to remember that the world needs to see the light of Christ in us, especially when times are tough.

Dear God, may I remind myself every day that your glory is present in me. Instead of feeling dejected or discouraged and bringing others down with me, I want to make a conscious choice to be a carrier of your glory and light. As I imagine myself bathed in your light, I thank you, God of light, for the privilege of allowing me to shine with your glory in the world. May I be aware of my role in every situation I encounter today.

Be Careful How You Live

Be careful then how you live, not as unwise people but as wise. . . .
So do not be foolish, but understand what the will of the Lord is.

—Ephesians 5:15, 17

Sometimes it's easier to just do what everyone else is doing. But that's not always the wisest choice. In fact, following the crowd without first following Jesus can lead us into bad times. Before we do what everyone else is doing, we need to ask ourselves how wise our behavior is or whether we understand what the will of God is for our lives. Perhaps we can ask ourselves this question: "Am I moving toward goodness, light, and love, or am I stumbling with others in the darkness?"

Light my path, dear Jesus, and help me to be wise rather than foolish. Wake me up to the fact that I can know whether I'm following your will by examining whether my choices and behaviors are filled with love and goodness. Remind me that I'm the one who must choose how I will behave. I don't have to thoughtlessly follow the crowd. I know that how I act will have an impact on how others choose to act. Make me a person who others will want to follow because following me will lead them to you.

CARRIED BY GOD

Even when you turn gray I will carry you.

—ISAIAH 46:4

How good it is to remind ourselves that we will never be abandoned, even when we grow old! Through the prophet Hosea, God tells us that it was he who taught us to walk when we were babies, who lifted us to his cheek and carried us (11:3-4). Then the prophet Isaiah tells us that God will not be put off by our gray hair or feeble ways. From the days when we were helpless infants through the difficulties and trials of old age, we can count on God's carrying us, his precious children, close to his heart.

God, you are my wonderful divine parent. I know that you value me, whatever my age or state in life. All of my days I am yours. Even when I cannot walk by myself, you will always "carry" me. I count on you to continue teaching me all the remaining months or years of my life. Let our time together lead me to total loving union with you.

OPEN YOUR HEART TO GOD

Open wide your hearts.

—2 CORINTHIANS 6:13

When we are troubled or perhaps even frightened, our natural inclination seems to be to close down and protect ourselves. We wrap ourselves in defensiveness and withdraw, trying to cover up our feelings of vulnerability. As we "batten down the hatches," we find ourselves in a darkness of our own creation. This is the very time when we need to open our hearts to God's light. His healing may come directly through prayer and the sacraments or through our loved ones who are reaching out to us. But healing will only come if our hearts are open to it.

God of everlasting love, I know that your heart is always open to me and to all of us. I can't imagine your closing off your heart to anyone. Help me to open my heart wide to you. I need your healing love to carry me through this difficult time. Let me be open to any way in which you choose to heal me.

The Blessing of Contentment

Be content with what you have.

—Hebrews 13:5

Often, instead of recognizing the abundance of what we have, we fret and strive for more. We have not only material possessions but also relationships, talents and abilities, and countless other blessings. Do we focus on our abundance or on our lack? When we think we don't have enough, we miss out on the peace of contentment and the delight of gratitude.

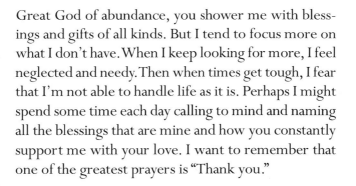

Great God of abundance, you shower me with blessings and gifts of all kinds. But I tend to focus more on what I don't have. When I keep looking for more, I feel neglected and needy. Then when times get tough, I fear that I'm not able to handle life as it is. Perhaps I might spend some time each day calling to mind and naming all the blessings that are mine and how you constantly support me with your love. I want to remember that one of the greatest prayers is "Thank you."

Sustaining the Weary

The Lord God has given me
the tongue of a teacher,
that I may know how to sustain
the weary with a word.

—Isaiah 50:4

How often in dark times do we find our greatest support and help in the loving words and presence of others? We have such power with each other when we reach out in love and care. Our good hearts give God the ability to be present in their suffering and to touch them through the personal warmth and caring words that we bring to them. May our actions and words bring sustenance to every person we meet.

What a privilege it is, dear loving God, when you choose to use me in your care of others! Use my tongue to speak words of compassion and support. Teach me how to be gentle and kind, and keep me from causing any distress or hurt. Let me see that while my words can be warm and helpful, so also can just my loving presence. Help me to be wise, and guide me as I reach out to people with your love.

Peace Begins with Me

Wisdom is better than weapons of war.
—Ecclesiastes 9:18

Jesus never suggested violence or war as a method to resolve a problem. In fact, even when he was in the midst of his approaching crucifixion, he never showed any signs of physical resistance. He never fought with those around him or suggested that anyone else fight. We must not view violence as a solution to our problems either. And even if we don't physically hurt someone, we need to be aware of our tone of voice, our gestures, and our words. Are we violent with others—or even with ourselves—when we are harsh or overly critical? May the peace of God reign in our hearts at all times.

Lord, I want peace to begin with me. I know that I can't build peace on earth unless I am at peace with myself. Make me aware of the times in my life when I can bring peace instead of violence to a situation. Let me rest in the peace of your Holy Spirit, and may I spread that peace to everyone I meet.

Deliver Me from All My Fears

I sought the LORD, and he answered me,
and delivered me from all my fears.

—Psalm 34:4

When things are falling apart, we sometimes hold back from making any effort to resolve the problem. We may fear failure, or we may lack the courage to step out and address the issue. We may even worry about how others will judge us or see us. That's when fear itself becomes a real handicap. Whenever we sense that fear in our hearts, we should seek the Lord. He can rescue us from our own fears and give us the courage we need to face any situation.

Help me, my powerful God, not to let my fears keep me from doing what I need to do. I need courage to confront the issues that overwhelm me. I believe that you will give me that courage. Let me be clear about my beliefs and strong in stepping out when I can help to resolve the turmoil in my life. Deliver me from fear, and give me the grace to trust you and your power in my life.

STOP BROODING OVER DAYS GONE BY

Stop dwelling on past events,
and brooding over days gone by.

—ISAIAH 43:18 (REB)

There is certainly profit to be gained by remembering the past—when we may have found new wisdom to live by, discovered hazards to avoid, or recognized blessings we hadn't seen before. When hard times or difficulties come into our minds, however, we may handicap ourselves by holding on to past events, perhaps blaming others or brooding over what went wrong. Then we give those past events the power to harm and embitter us rather than helping us. The best way to deal with our past is to glean the wisdom of the experience, grieve as necessary, learn from our mistakes, and move on.

When I've been injured or hurt by any events or people in my life, instead of brooding over the ill or unfair treatment and feeling sorry for myself, let me sit with you, my loving God, and think about what I might gain from the experience. Guide me through the hard times, the pain, and the feelings of anger and hurt so that I might grieve if necessary and be able to let it go. If there is something I can learn from the experience, show me. When I catch myself brooding and feeling bad, help me turn to you to find the gift that this experience holds for me.

God Keeps His Promises

He has said, "I will never leave you or forsake you."
So we can say with confidence,
"The Lord is my helper;
I will not be afraid.
What can anyone do to me?"

—Hebrews 13:5-6

Our problems sometimes come from ascribing our human ways to God. Because we tend to not be trustworthy or to not say what we mean, we think God acts in the same way. But when God says, "I will never leave you or forsake you," he means just that! Perhaps we need to remind ourselves daily of this promise, especially when we feel afraid.

I will affirm every day this promise that you have made to me: "I will never leave you or forsake you." As I repeat these words, I strengthen my trust and also remind myself of what I know to be true. Then, in the times when I find myself feeling worried, afraid, or alone, I will simply repeat the same words several times over, reinforcing what I already believe.

Our Special Gifts

Each of us has been given a special gift,
a particular share in the bounty of Christ.

—Ephesians 4:7 (REB)

When life presents us with big challenges and times become difficult, our sense of ineptness and helplessness threatens to take over. We feel incompetent and unable to deal with or solve our problems. In the midst of such hard times, we need to remind ourselves that we are not helpless. To be truly humble means to know that we each have a unique and special way to be the vehicle through which God operates in this world. We need to agree to offer ourselves for the healing of the world, each in our own way.

Be present in me, my God, so that through me, you can be present in the midst of the trials and problems I encounter. Show me that I'm not helpless. Make me aware of the unique ways and gifts I have that you want to use. I offer myself to you so that you can work through me. What a blessing it is for me when you use me to be here for others. May I never underestimate my gifts. May I always be grateful for each one of them.

Praying in the Darkness

*In the morning, while it was still very dark, he got up and went
out to a deserted place, and there he prayed.*

—Mark 1:35

Jesus was willing to walk right into the darkness of night and
pray, knowing that the light would come. How well his actions
can speak to us in our times of darkness. Avoiding the darkness
may be impossible. Even in the natural world, we cycle through
the light and darkness of the day and night. Perhaps by following
Jesus' example, we can bring ourselves to pray in whatever dark
situations we experience, knowing that light will come.

Here I am, Lord, sitting with you in the midst of my
hard times. Just knowing that you are here reassures
me that this darkness will end and the light will come.
Just being aware that I'm here with you is a profound
prayer for me. No words are necessary as I sit close
to you and experience the warmth, beauty, and care
of your presence.

SHELTER ME, O GOD

Trust in him at all times, O people;
pour out your heart before him;
God is a refuge for us.

—PSALM 62:8

Life can make us victims at times, and we have no way of avoiding that. We may also make choices that we later regret, or perhaps others have made choices that affect us negatively. Loss and misfortune happen in everyone's life. So even when we do all the "right things," we may still find ourselves suffering and in distress. In such situations the psalmist offers two significant suggestions. First, tell God about your troubles by pouring out your heart. Second, trust that even before you had asked for help, God was holding you in his loving care. He is your shelter and refuge.

Dear God, in my distress I know that you love me and are with me. You are sheltering me, holding me close to your heart. I know that many of my struggles are simply some of the painful realities of life that everyone experiences from time to time. I also know that pouring out my heart to you is a wonderful way of letting go of my pain. Telling you all about it helps me to release my burdens to you. I trust that you will soothe my pain and comfort me.

DON'T LOSE HEART

So we do not lose heart. Even though our outer nature is wasting away, our inner nature is being renewed day by day.

—2 CORINTHIANS 4:16

In our lives we experience renewal and loss, hope and discouragement. This is the rhythm of life, the very nature of our existence. Yet in the difficult times, we can be tempted to give up—to lose heart. When interviewed on the occasion of his eightieth birthday, Holocaust survivor and author Viktor Frankl was asked about what he had learned during his struggles and trials in a concentration camp. He noted that everything can be taken from us but one thing: our response to a situation, and the attitude we bring to it.

Lord, when I'm tempted to lose heart in the difficulties of my life, remind me that I have choices—that I can choose, with your help, not to give up. Help me to remember that no one else "makes" me react in any particular way. I have the freedom to choose my response. I want to choose life and hope, even when times are tough. I want to remember that everything—even my difficulties—can lead me to you, my loving God.

You Are God's Temple

Surely you know that you are God's temple, where the spirit of God dwells. . . . For the temple of God is holy; and you are that temple.
—1 Corinthians 3:16-17 (REB)

How awesome it is for us to be aware of this reality: that each of us is the temple of God, the place where God manifests himself in this world. The Spirit of God is alive in us! When we give our very being to God, he will use us to accomplish amazing things. When times are problematic, it's important to keep that reality always in front of us. With God working in us, we will have the strength and courage to be all that we can be.

I need to bask in the awareness of the blessing that God is using me. God is living and breathing in me and working through me to touch my problems and those around me. What a huge gift—to be the vehicle that God needs to accomplish his work in the world! I want to be a willing cooperator with God. This temple that carries my name is holy.

Peace at All Times

Now may the Lord of peace himself give you peace at all times in all ways. The Lord be with all of you.

—2 Thessalonians 3:16

What is it about peace that makes it so important spiritually? All through the Scriptures, we find greetings such as "Peace be with you." How many times did Jesus himself reach out to those in distress with blessings of peace? When the storm whipped up on the Sea of Galilee and Jesus was sleeping in the boat, his apostles were terrified and called for him to save them. Jesus' words to the sea were ones of peace: "Peace! Be still!" (Mark 4:39). Only when we're at peace can we deal reasonably with our distress.

Jesus, maybe when I sit down to pray, or even when I'm in the midst of difficulties in my life, I need to take a deep breath and say to myself the words you said to the storming sea: "Peace! Be still!" Being still seems to be a prerequisite for being in touch with you, dear Jesus. May I do so!

The Power of Words

She opens her mouth with wisdom,
and the teaching of kindness is on her tongue.

—Proverbs 31:26

How frequently throughout the Scriptures are we warned of the great damage we can do to others by what comes out of our mouths! The Book of Proverbs describes the qualities of an ideal wife, which include the wisdom and kindness of her speech. She is a model for all of us, both men and women alike. She teaches us the importance of encouraging others rather than criticizing them. When times are difficult, we may find ourselves making the situation worse by the words we use. We must be cautious about our own speech at such times, and also avoid others whose words tend to bring us down.

Jesus, Word of God, let my speech be a way in which you can influence your people through me. May I always speak kindly to whomever I encounter. Let me never speak destructively of others or gossip about them. I know I have the power to bring good or ill simply by what I say. Help me to bring love, kindness, and wisdom, not negativity, criticism, or complaint.

Where Can I Go?

Where can I go from your spirit?
Or where can I flee from your presence?

—Psalm 139:7

In the comic strips of our early days, when life got tough, the characters would pack up their belongings and run away from home. So often we have the same inclination to run. We may want to run from our problems so that we won't have to face what's hard for us or the poor choices we've made. But it's impossible to run away from God. After all, he is the One who made us and in whose tender, loving, and healing hands our lives continue to be held. And with compassion and love, he will help us "stay at home" to face our problems and poor choices.

Creator and loving God, it was your love for me that brought me into existence and continues to hold me here, wrapped in your warmth and care. You know every detail of my life—the things I'm proud of and the things I regret. It helps me to remind myself that you haven't given up on me and have no intention of doing so. Let me picture myself being held closely in your loving embrace. I don't want to flee from your presence or your love for me.

Facing the Darkness

Take no part in the unfruitful works of darkness.

—Ephesians 5:11

Unlike a seed that waits and grows to wholeness in the underground darkness of fertile soil, darkness may also be used as a hiding place for less wholesome activities. We may choose to use darkness as a way of avoiding or refusing to face our difficulties. We pretend our problems and difficulties don't exist, or we cover them up with denial and ignorance and other unhealthy actions and thoughts. Unfortunately, when we do this, we may wind up with more trouble.

Jesus, you told us to be "children of light" (John 12:36). Walk with me into my dark places, and help me to be willing to face them. Help me to find the wisdom waiting for me when I stop avoiding problems. When I face them with you at my side, my times of darkness can be fruitful and full of blessing for me. Help me discover the lessons or gifts that my problems hold. May I find your life and your blessings in the darkness that I was afraid to face on my own.

ASK FOR FAITH

"Whatever you ask for in prayer with faith, you will receive."
—MATTHEW 21:22

When we read these words of Jesus, we expect that whatever we ask for will be ours. If that doesn't happen, we may complain and become disheartened. We may even be tempted to believe that his words are not true. But perhaps instead of asking for something specific, we should ask for an increase in faith. God can give us the grace to know, without a doubt, that he hears our pleas from the depths of our being and that he won't allow anything that is not in our best interest. What a gift that is!

Loving God, I trust that what you give me must be just what I need. It may look nothing like what I had asked for. But let my faith be great enough that I can truly thank you for what comes, knowing that you did hear me and simply "adjusted" your answer to my prayer in a way that I would be blessed.

Turn to Me

Turn to me and be gracious to me,
for I am lonely and afflicted.
Relieve the troubles of my heart,
and bring me out of my distress.

—Psalm 25:16-17

When we're lonely and afflicted, how might God bring us out of our distress? Sometimes the very distress or difficulty we are experiencing can be the seed out of which growth or help comes. God may want us to take an honest look at ourselves and our situation so that he can show us the true source of our troubles. Perhaps some unhealthy behaviors or thought patterns are causing some of our problems, or perhaps we are responding to a loved one in an unproductive or unkind way. The Lord's light of healing will emerge from the shadows as I look to him, for he is a gracious God.

Please, God, help me to examine the troubles of my heart so that I can understand just what is so troubling to me. I know that new life can be born out of the seeds of my distress. Show me where I need to change, and nourish that new life in me.

A Model for Others

Show yourself in all respects a model of good works.

—TITUS 2:7

As the old adage says, "Actions speak louder than words." The most profound way we can proclaim our belief in God and teach others is by what we do. We all speak loudly through our behavior—how we live each day, the choices we make, and how we treat one another. So when times are difficult, our best course of action is to be strong, loving, faithful, and trusting, and to live with integrity.

Jesus, you described yourself as "the way." You are the model for us all. Help me follow you in good times and in bad. Together we can be strong models for others so that they will be supported, guided, and encouraged in their own journeys. As I walk with you, we can clear the path for all those who come after us.

Pursue What Makes for Peace

*Let us then pursue what makes for peace
and for mutual upbuilding.*

—Romans 14:19

What if in the midst of conflict, we chose to make peace instead of war? What if we put all our energies and wisdom into mapping out a strategy that would benefit those on both sides of the struggle? No one on either side of the conflict would die in the effort or be injured or maimed. Both sides would work toward "mutual upbuilding." In every situation that involves conflict and the battling of wills, let us pursue what makes for peace, not war.

Dear Lord, I want to contribute all my skills, knowledge, and effort to building up the peace and unity of your creation. I want to be instrumental in bringing about your peace and love in my own struggles and those around me. I don't want to be divisive and negative. Lord, make me an instrument of your peace.

Watch Out for Blind Guides

"If one blind man guides another,
they will both fall into the ditch."

—Matthew 15:14 (REB)

How many times do we get to the wrong place in life because we follow the wrong leader? So much advice comes to us from so many sources. Sometimes we are attracted to someone else's lifestyle and want to imitate it. We may get caught up in "peer pressure" and reflexively decide to do something because everyone else is doing it. Instead, we need to step back and discern what's motivating us to do certain things. If we first pray for wisdom and ask God to steer us, he will lead us in the way we should go.

Holy Spirit, give me eyes to see how I might be moving in the wrong direction. Help me to pick my guides clearly and well. I want to follow godly people who put you first and help me to do the same. Fill me with your wisdom so that I'm a good guide for others when they come to me for help or advice.

LOOKING FOR JESUS

And when they looked up, they saw no one except Jesus himself.
—MATTHEW 17:8

We know that Jesus is with us and in us at all times. So in every situation in which we find ourselves, wouldn't it be wonderful if we were able to "look up" and know that Jesus is there? Whatever our circumstances, we can make it our aim to always seek him out. He is truly part of every person and situation. We can develop the habit of "looking" for Jesus—in good times and in bad. What a gift it would be to be able to sense his presence in every moment of the day.

Jesus, in every challenge, let this be my prayer: "Lord, where are you? Help me to find you in this situation." Show me how I might be in touch with you. I know that I am not alone. Help me to get into the habit of "looking up" and seeing no one but you.

THE MUSIC OF THE NATURAL WORLD

Sing for joy, O heavens, and exult, O earth;
break forth, O mountains, into singing!
For the LORD has comforted his people,
and will have compassion on his suffering ones.

—ISAIAH 49:13

When our days are dark and we feel defeated by our hard times, we tend to walk blindly through our lives, not seeing the gifts of the beautiful earth around us. Some of our greatest solace and healing can be found in the music of the natural world, if only we open our ears to hear it. The mountains, the songs of the birds, the warmth of the sunshine, or the coolness of the breeze comforts and blesses us. But we must be open to receive these gifts—and even to see them as the gifts that they are!

Thank you for the healing gifts of this earth, Creator God. Help me to open my eyes and consciously notice what's around me. Help me feel the warmth of your presence in the sunshine. Help me hear the birds singing their songs for me. Let me smell the fragrance of the flowers. Let me realize that you use all of creation to tell me how much you love me. Your radiant presence is everywhere. Open my eyes and ears!

Do You Want to Be Healed?

"Do you want to be made well?"

—John 5:6

How often are we in trouble because we've exonerated ourselves from any responsibility for our own lives? When that happens, our problems simply hang on, along with the pain that comes with them. We continue to wallow in our troubles, believing that there's no way out. We feel helpless and lose hope, thinking that things can never change. First we have to ask ourselves the question that Jesus posed to the afflicted man sitting by the pool of Bethsaida: "Do you want to be made well?"

Jesus, heal me. My life has been very hard at times, and I haven't always been proactive in seeking solutions or owning up to my own mistakes. But I do want to be made well. Instead of holding on to the mistaken belief that I'll never get out of my difficulties, I want to choose life and healing. Give me the grace and the help that I need. Send those into my life who will support me. Enable me to continue to say yes to you and your healing and goodness.

Wrapped in God's Peace

*"Peace I leave with you; my peace I give to you.
I do not give to you as the world gives. Do not let your hearts
be troubled, and do not let them be afraid."*

—JOHN 14:27

How often do we find ourselves facing trouble at every turn?
Turmoil can permeate every aspect of our lives—our personal
relationships, our finances, our health, our jobs. And even when
only one aspect of our lives is in disorder, it can often affect other
areas. In the same way, one troubled relationship can affect our
other relationships. How desperately we need God's help to find
personal and mutual peace. When we find ourselves in such turmoil and at war within ourselves or with others, we need to rely
on Jesus' promise to give us his peace.

Jesus, help me to learn to contribute to the building up of peace in myself and in my world. I know
that I can't isolate one area of my life from the others. When I'm not feeling peaceful, it affects other
parts of my life or other relationships. I want to be
an agent of new life, peace, and growth in all that I
do and say. I believe you will give me the peace that I
am asking for if I sit with you today. Wrap me in your
peace, dear Lord.

Goodness Can Prevail

There must be no limit to your goodness,
as your heavenly father's goodness knows no bounds.
—Matthew 5:48 (REB)

When times are difficult and we struggle to deal with them, our inclination is to feel assaulted and to strike out at those around us. When we attack each other and point fingers, blaming one another, the situation only intensifies. Nothing good happens in such times. Each of us must choose to respond peacefully and lovingly rather than reacting with bitterness, anger, or resentment. Only we can change negative situations into places where goodness prevails.

God of goodness and peace, when times are tough, I want to choose the peaceful, loving way. I don't want to add hatred and negativity to any problem, which can only stir up more trouble. Help me to be a witness for peace and goodness.

You Are Precious

Do not fear, for I have redeemed you;
I have called you by name, you are mine.
When you pass through the waters, I will be with you; . . .
Because you are precious in my sight,
and honored, and I love you.

—Isaiah 43:1-2, 4

Imagine the great God of all creation, telling each of us how precious we are! He also tells us how uniquely we are loved—each of us is known by name! God wants us to know that when frightening things happen to us, we need not fear—we are wrapped in our Father's love and protection.

O God, who created me and who still finds me "precious," even after years of my being less than I could be, I am astounded by your love for me! Thank you for choosing to create me and for telling me how much you love me. Help me to love you with all my heart, mind, soul, and strength. Give me a grateful heart that never forgets your love for me.

SHOW KINDNESS

Never neglect to show kindness and to share what you have with others, for such are the sacrifices which God approves.
—HEBREWS 13:16 (REB)

Reaching out to others with kindness and care can provide them with just what they need to deal with the stresses and hard times in their lives. Sometimes sharing something we have already struggled with can be the turning point in their own struggles, giving them the wisdom, insight, and encouragement they need to be able to cope. Through each of us, God can reach into the lives of others and bring blessings.

Generous and loving God, thank you for letting me participate when you want to help my brothers and sisters in need. Use my willingness to be kind as your avenue to touch others. Show me how I can share the gifts that life has given to me with someone else. I know that when I allow you to use me to bless others, I will surely be blessed as well—more than I can imagine. What an opportunity for me!

Casting Out Demons

*That evening, at sunset, they brought to him all who were sick
or possessed with demons. And the whole city was gathered
around the door. And he cured many who were sick with
various diseases, and cast out many demons.*

—Mark 1:32-34

It seems that none of us is without "demons"—St. Mark notes
that the "whole city" gathered around the door where Jesus was.
Some "demons" have come into our lives through poor choices,
laziness, or an unwillingness to take responsibility for our lives.
Others afflict us through no fault of our own. So when we find
ourselves in the midst of difficulties, we begin to address them by
acknowledging our need and naming our demons. Only when we
name them can we come to see how they are bringing us down.
Then we can work toward turning them around by taking responsibility for our own choices and asking for help. Only in this way
do we have a chance to be "cured."

If I had lived two thousand years ago, I would have
wanted to be in the middle of that crowd, "around the
door" where you were, Jesus. However, even though
I wasn't there, I am here, and so are you. And you
have the same power and ability now to cure my problems and evict my demons as you had then. Help me
to begin to name my demons. If you help me name
them and own up to them, I'm sure that together we
can "cast them out."

YOU ARE NOT ALONE

Do not be far from me,
for trouble is near
and there is no one to help.

—PSALM 22:11

Have you ever felt all alone in your difficulties? Perhaps family problems or issues at work are throwing you out of kilter, and you feel as if you have no one to turn to. Maybe you can't see a way out of your problems and lose hope that anyone can help you. In such times we must remember that we aren't alone. God is always with us, ready to hear our cries of distress. He may even help us to remember that there are friends and family who love us and want to help us. Truly, we are not alone!

God, I know I am not alone because you are close to me. Let me tell you, one by one, what my worries are. You will listen to me, and I will spend time in silence listening to a word from you. And, dear God, if there is someone I'm forgetting who can help me, please bring that person to mind. I know you want what is best for me. Bring me healing, light, and love.

Speaking Prudently

To watch over mouth and tongue
is to keep out of trouble.

—Proverbs 21:23

How often do we find ourselves wishing that we hadn't said something! Once the words are out of our mouths, however, we can't take them back. Sometimes we tend to speak too quickly and impulsively, without first thinking about the impact of our words and our tone of voice. Perhaps we can decide to hold our tongue until we're sure we can stand behind what we say. Speaking without being prudent and judicious may cause us to regret our words—and arouse unnecessary division and strife.

Keep me out of trouble, dear God of wisdom. Help me to pause and consider what I plan to say before I create trouble for everyone, including myself. Perhaps that moment of silence will help me to speak with love and concern rather than with judgment or criticism.

A Grateful Heart

Persevere in prayer, with minds alert and with thankful hearts.
—Colossians 4:2 (REB)

It's often difficult to feel gratitude toward God when we are in the midst of painful or troubling times. Yet getting into the habit of saying "Thank you" can help us in more ways than we could possibly imagine. A grateful heart lifts our spirits. It makes us think of other blessings that we may forget when we are focusing only on our troubles. And thanking God in advance builds our trust in him. The thirteenth-century German mystic Meister Eckhart once said, "If the only prayer you ever say in your entire life is 'Thank you,' it will be enough."

Blessed God, I want to always be confident in advance that you are and will be helping me with my troubles. So I thank you in advance for all your gifts, knowing they often bring me blessings, even when I don't think they will. I even thank you for my troubles, because I know that some good will come out of them. I give you thanks with all my heart, trusting in your wisdom and love.

BLESSED ARE THE PEACEMAKERS

"Blessed are the peacemakers, for they will be called children of God."
—MATTHEW 5:9

When things get difficult and struggle is the order of the day, we tend to experience little peace. Yet how many times did Jesus encourage us to strive for peace? And how often did he greet people with these words: "Peace be with you." We know that when we are in turmoil, it tends to be contagious, causing those around us to join in our distress. Yet we're so influenced by one another that peace can be contagious too. When the world is in turmoil and we choose peace, we are choosing to be children of God.

Dear Jesus, like you I want to hold my heart in peacefulness so that anyone who encounters me may be drawn into that peace. Keep me conscious of how much we all influence one another. Help me to be aware that I can choose to create a peaceful environment—one that affects all who are with me—even when times are difficult.

LOVE ONE ANOTHER

"This is my commandment, that you love
one another as I have loved you."

—JOHN 15:12

How rapidly our world can change! Everything may be going well, and then something happens, and we find ourselves in a great deal of distress. But whatever the situation, we have a profound influence on each other—often without realizing it. No matter what we're experiencing, our love for one another is the key. How important it is for each of us to recognize the power we have to build up or to tear down by what we say or do. Jesus' commandment to each one of us is crystal clear: "Love one another." Whatever we're feeling or whatever difficulty we're in, we can still choose to be loving.

Jesus, you've not only told us but you've also shown us what it means to love. Please help me to understand how important is the love I have to give. Help me be a positive and loving person to everyone I encounter, even when I don't agree with the other person's ideas, and help me choose not to act in ways that are destructive. Each time I choose to love, I further your love in the world. No matter what I come up against, help me choose to be loving and life-giving.

Draw Near to God

Draw near to God, and he will draw near to you.

—James 4:8

We know in our hearts that God is closer to us than we can even begin to imagine. St. Augustine said that God is closer to us than we are to ourselves! And yet we almost never consciously and purposefully remind ourselves of that truth. We therefore miss out on the comfort and support we could experience, especially in times of distress, and spend our time in purposeless fretting and worry.

What delight I would have if I could begin to train my mind to consciously think of you and how present you are to me, my God. You want to be with me and you want me to know how much you care for me. When I don't choose to "draw near" to you, I miss the wonderful conscious awareness of your presence "right here" with me.

Gifts in the Darkness

Even the darkness is not dark to you;
the night is as bright as the day,
for darkness is as light to you.

—Psalm 139:12

If we seek the wisdom of our circumstances and experiences, we might find that even hard things, such as darkness, have gifts to offer. Frequently, it's our hardest times that teach us the most, or that bring about the most growth in us. Often we see this in retrospect, when we can look back and see how we've changed for the better. When we trust in God being with us in the darkness, we will never be disappointed.

Wake me up, dear Spirit of God, to the fact that everything in my life can teach me and bring me wisdom. May I find that even the difficult times of darkness carry within them a seed that can develop in me and bring me to new life and growth in you. Help me to be open so that I can find and welcome the gifts you have for me.

Hold Fast to Love

But as for you, return to your God,
hold fast to love and justice,
and wait continually for your God.

—Hosea 12:6

How easy it is for us to get lost and wander into ways that get us nowhere. We can go deeper into a darkness of poor and unhelpful choices that become unhealthy habits. Instead of supporting us with our problems and helping us find our way, these habits add another unhealthy dimension to the darkness in which we find ourselves, leading us away from God's love and care. At such times we must remember that God isn't lost—we are. If we recognize our plight, we must also know that we can make a choice to return. So hold fast to love. Call on God to return and help you, and know that your God will appear.

Loving God, come and find me. I'm waiting here in a darkness of my own making, and I need you to rescue me. I've gotten myself into a tight spot, and only you can release me. I am sorry for having wandered so far from you. I trust in your power and love. Stay close so that I do not get lost again. I want to be close to you always.

Don't Be Anxious about Tomorrow

*"So do not be anxious about tomorrow; tomorrow will look after
itself. Each day has troubles enough of its own."*
—Matthew 6:34 (REB)

We can spend so much time focused and worrying about the hard
times that might happen in the future that we fail to live fully in
the only time we ever have: right now. Not only do we struggle
with what might happen, but we may even be tempted to magnify
those problems in our minds. It can be helpful to prepare for the
future when we have the resources to address a particular issue.
But we must avoid letting our fear and anxiety feed our imagina-
tion so that every issue looms larger than it really is or ever will
be. Living as well as we can, in every moment of every day, may
be our best way of addressing our anxiety for the future.

In every single moment of my life, you are here, my
ever-present and nurturing Lord. You know my problems before I do. Help me to focus on you when
I'm worried instead of fretting over what might happen. I want to always remember that this "now" is the
moment in which you live and love me. Let me deal
with my upset by giving over each moment to you.

JESUS WEPT

When Jesus saw her weeping, and the Jews who came
with her also weeping, he was greatly disturbed in spirit
and deeply moved. . . . Jesus began to weep.

—JOHN 11:33, 35

How touched and deeply affected Jesus was with the death of his friend, Lazarus, and with the grief and sadness of Lazarus' sisters and friends. How like us Jesus was as he faced the sadness and troubles of this world. In expressing the deep grief he felt, he showed us how to deal in a healthy, holy way with the losses and sorrow in our own lives. Grief is one of the most painful experiences we can have. Jesus shows us that it's perfectly human to express our grief by expressing it outwardly. By doing so, we are able to take the first step in coping with the loss.

Jesus, my brother, you showed me how to grieve the loss of those who are dear and important to me. You showed me that expressing my own sadness and distress can help me appreciate the gift of the one I've lost in death. Only in this way can I live through the loss and find my joy again. Thank you for your gift of the one I've lost, and thank you for showing me your own tender heart and how willing you were to grieve.

Faithful Friends Are a Treasure

Faithful friends are a sturdy shelter:
whoever finds one has found a treasure.

—Sirach 6:14

An old adage says that a good friend can double our delight and halve our sorrow. Struggling with our difficulties on our own can make us feel lonely, trapped, and inept. We fear that we'll never find our way through them. The presence of a true and faithful friend, with good values and genuine care for us, can be a wonderful way in which we can actually experience God present in our lives.

Loving God, thank you for being my best friend, and thank you for the truly good friends you've brought into my life. May we be good, faithful, and supportive friends to each other, especially when either of us is caught in the midst of painful and difficult times. Remind me that I can also choose to be a good friend to myself.

Nothing Is Too Hard for God

*Ah Lord God! It is you who made the heavens and
the earth by your great power and by your outstretched arm!
Nothing is too hard for you.*

—Jeremiah 32:17

Despair may overwhelm us at times, when all of life feels painful and we fear that we'll never find our way out of the darkness. These are the times when we must remind ourselves that the God who made the heavens and the earth is still with us, holding us in his "outstretched arms" when we feel helpless. Remember that "nothing is too hard" for our God!

Great God of power and might, I am so helpless without you. But I am never without you! Let me see that if I align myself with you, nothing is too hard. So I invite you into my distress and darkness and ask you to hold me close. Turn my despair into trust in you, and support me with your power.

Learning from Our Blindness

Out of their gloom and darkness
the eyes of the blind shall see.

—Isaiah 29:18

Sometimes we don't realize that the very darkness itself, or the things that we find problematic and distressing, is the ground out of which we will find our wisdom and answers. Many times Jesus spoke of our having eyes but not seeing. Perhaps if we look in a new and open way at the darkness—the very things over which we stumble—we'll find an answer we didn't anticipate. Maybe our blindness isn't permanent, and can actually teach us a lot.

My loving God, you are the God of darkness as well as of light. So you are here in all of my times of darkness, holding some gift, some wisdom for me to find. I may be amazed at finding wisdom in such an unexpected place, but if you are here, so is your wisdom. Help me to always look for it so that I don't miss the gift.

GOD IS OUR REFUGE

Trust in him at all times, O people;
pour out your heart before him;
God is a refuge for us."

—PSALM 62:8

Sometimes we can feel weighed down by worry and distress, not only for our own problems, but for those of the world. Perhaps the difficulties we have with a relationship reflect the tensions and conflicts in society today. Perhaps as we struggle with our own financial hardships, we worry about those who live in such poverty that they don't have food to eat or a place to live. Maybe our health issues are even a greater challenge for those without access to care. All these problems may seem insurmountable at times. We ache for peace and constantly look for a place of refuge that we can count on. But as the psalmist knew so well, God is our refuge and our strength. He invites us to pour out the burdens in our hearts to him.

So many times when I'm distressed, O Lord, I find solace in being able to pour out my heart to a dear friend. Just telling my story or talking about my worries can help me find some peace and even at times find solutions. I want to pour out my heart to you with no holding back. I want to trust in your love for me and your help in my own distress and in that of our world. Lighten our hearts, and give us hope that in you we can resolve our difficulties.

Love Covers All Offenses

Hatred stirs up strife,
but love covers all offenses.

—Proverbs 10:12

We can exacerbate our difficulties by the choices we make to deal with them. When we choose to emphasize the negative and problematic, we introduce anger, resentment, bitterness, and even hatred into our relationships and our situations. When we choose to bring love, we begin the process of healing and resolution.

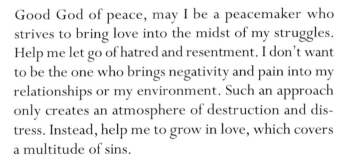

Good God of peace, may I be a peacemaker who strives to bring love into the midst of my struggles. Help me let go of hatred and resentment. I don't want to be the one who brings negativity and pain into my relationships or my environment. Such an approach only creates an atmosphere of destruction and distress. Instead, help me to grow in love, which covers a multitude of sins.

DOING WHAT WE CAN

Then you shall call, and the LORD will answer;
you shall cry for help, and he will say, Here I am.
If you remove the yoke from among you,
the pointing of the finger, the speaking of evil,
if you offer your food to the hungry
and satisfy the needs of the afflicted,
then your light shall rise in the darkness
and your gloom be like the noonday.

—ISAIAH 58:9-10

There are many ways we might contribute to resolving the difficulties around us. If we address some of our omissions, we may just find some of those problems abating. Are we helping to care for the afflicted? Do we reach out and call for God's help, even as we offer our own gifts, talents, and energy to solve a problem? It's too easy to feel helpless and inept or to blame others when we may be at least partially responsible. That allows us to stand back and let others get involved when we could be doing some of the heavy lifting ourselves.

Merciful God, I'm just one person, and the problems I see around me are large and seemingly unsolvable. Yet through you I know that I can do my part in addressing them. I want to be like the noonday sun, rising as light in the darkness. Help me to know what I can do, and then help me to do it!

I Am with You Always

"And remember, I am with you always, to the end of the age."
—Matthew 28:20

We are much more likely to be able to cope with our problems when we know that we have some support. When we stand alone in the face of difficulty, we feel threatened and overwhelmed and too weak and helpless to make any impact. Even when we know we're on the side of truth, we falter when we feel that no one is standing with us. St. Matthew gives us the words that the risen Jesus uttered after his terrible battle with darkness and death. Jesus promises to be our support for as long as time exists.

Jesus, help me take your words to heart. Each morning when I wake up to a new day, help me to call to mind your words and know that they are meant for me that very day. I believe you. I want to remind myself each morning to look for you and to count on your care for me. I know that you are also with me through the love and support of my friends and loved ones. Help me to keep that awareness alive throughout the day.

Dwelling Places

Do not let your hearts be troubled. Believe in God, believe also in
me. In my Father's house there are many dwelling places.

—John 14:1-2

Life can be so problematic that our hearts may spend a fair
amount of time being "troubled." Yet Jesus suggested that there
might be other ways to deal with our troubles, such as believing in him as well as his Father—and trusting that help is always
close at hand. Perhaps that's what he meant by "many dwelling
places." Some of the places we can choose to dwell in to help us
with our troubled hearts might be quiet prayer, meditation, or
talking over our distress with a friend, a counselor, or a spiritual
director. Each of these opportunities can be one of those places
where God dwells.

I bring my troubled heart to you, my loving God, in
the quiet of this spot where I know you are waiting
for me. I sit with you and breathe slowly and deeply,
releasing my worry and anxiety with each breath.
I tell you about my distress, knowing that you are
holding me close to your heart. I let myself feel the
warmth of your presence and the love you have for
me. Help me remember the beauty of this encounter, and inspire me to return to this place often with
you. I know I can always find you here.

BLESS THOSE WHO CURSE YOU

"Bless those who curse you, pray for those who abuse you."

—LUKE 6:28

All too often we find that other people are at the crux of our own hard times. For one reason or another, relationships fall apart. Unkindness, miscommunications, and misunderstandings cause rifts in friendships. Words are spoken that attack and hurt, and we feel the need to defend ourselves and retaliate. We each know that we are "right" and the other person is "wrong." So the battle continues, and all "sides" are affected and can be damaged in the process. What a unique idea Jesus brings to the fray! Instead of keeping the battle going, he asks for blessing and prayer. It doesn't seem to matter who is right or who is wrong. He tells us to bless even those who curse us and pray for those who may be abusing us. Both sides must bring blessing and prayer into the situation.

Dear God of peace, I'm sure there have been many times when I've acted self-righteously and was heavily critical of others. I may have even been "right" but acted in an unkind or abusive way to the one who disagreed with me. Yet I know what Jesus wants me to do. Help me to be a peacemaker and to find a way to coexist lovingly with others, even when my feelings, thoughts, and beliefs are different from others. Perhaps then we will all be blessed.

Seeing beneath the Surface

"Do you have eyes, and fail to see?"

—Mark 8:18

More often than not, we get caught up in seeing things in limited ways. How many times did Jesus tell us to look beyond the surface? We can be so overwhelmed by our difficulties and problems that we don't look more deeply at the situations we're in. When we do probe more deeply, we may find that God is with us, giving us hope and a way out of our troubles.

May I learn how to really see, my God, so that I can find you hidden in the situations that trip me up. Let my inner eyes be opened, and may I be willing to really look. Maybe then I'll find that you and your strength and knowledge give me many reasons to hope. Fill me always with the hope that can come only from you.

I Will Give You Rest

*"Come to me, all you that are weary and are
carrying heavy burdens, and I will give you rest."*

—Matthew 11:28

One doesn't live very long in this world without experiencing heaviness and distress. We can feel desperate for rest and support as we stumble and even fall. The weariness we can sometimes feel may even tempt us to give up hope. Sickness, death, sorrow, and fear—all have a part to play in the human condition. Jesus experienced those things firsthand, and when we are in similar circumstances, he calls us to himself. As he stumbled with his cross, he reached out for help. He continues to be present in our lives, calling us to come to him for help and support.

Jesus, my brother, my God, help me. I don't think I can continue to battle this heaviness and darkness without you. Hold me up. Hold me close to you. Let me feel the support of your strength wrapping around me. I am weary, and my load is so heavy. Hold me and comfort me!

What Does God Wants from Us?

He has told you, O mortal, what is good;
and what does the LORD require of you
but to do justice, and to love kindness,
and to walk humbly with your God?

—Micah 6:8

We often feel unsure of what God wants from us. In troubling times, we assume that we should make big sacrifices. We promise to fast and deny ourselves. We think that by doing so, we can "even out" the exchange: If we "offer up" enough, we'll surely receive what we ask for. And to this God says: "Be kind and just. That is the 'fast' that I want. And know the truth of who you are and who I am."

I notice, my God, that you aren't only asking me to be just and kind but to love the kindness that I bring to my encounters. So let me be aware that grudging kindness is a terribly poor substitute for genuine loving care. Help me to grow in a warm and humble awareness of what part I can play in difficult interactions. If I choose to be kind, perhaps it will help others bring the same healing qualities to those they encounter each day.

Be Still and Know God

"Be still, and know that I am God!"

—Psalm 46:10

When times are difficult and challenges are all around us, we can get so frazzled and anxious that we do things impulsively and make things worse. Maybe the first thing we need to do is ground ourselves by remembering that there is someone who can give us insight into handling our problem. There is someone we can trust who has brought us through difficult times in the past. So perhaps when troubles overwhelm us, we should first sit quietly and remember the awesome power of the God who loves us and is only waiting for us to come to him.

Beloved God, I'm able to find you better when I quiet down and remember how close you are. You are in the stillness around me and within me. Bring me to a place of peace, and let me remember that you are ever holding me close. In my quietness I trust that you will guide me in doing whatever I can to resolve my distress. I want to stay here awhile, be still, and rest in the quietness that is you.

A SACRIFICE OF PRAISE

I call upon you, O LORD; come quickly to me;
give ear to my voice when I call to you.
Let my prayer be counted as incense before you,
and the lifting up of my hands as an evening sacrifice.

—PSALM 141:1-2

Every prayer we offer should be a sign of our praise, respect, and love for God. As we pray, we can imagine a cloud of incense rising from our hearts, in which is nestled our love and praise and our call for help, all rising together as we anticipate God's response. As we lift our hands to the Lord, let us imagine that we are holding up the needs of the whole world. Then we can ask God to hear us, help us, and receive our love and gratitude.

My loving God, let my prayer rise as incense before you. Let it be filled with my love and praise. When I hold up my hands to you, I would like you to see in them everyone for whom I've promised to pray. All of us are in great need of prayer and healing, Lord, so come quickly!

Choose Life

I have set before you life and death, blessings and curses. Choose life so that you and your descendants may live, loving the Lord your God, obeying him, and holding fast to him.

—Deuteronomy 30:19-20

Every day of our lives we have choices to make, choices that bring life or death, blessings or curses. These choices become more obvious when our lives are troubled. Our inclination during difficult times is toward blaming and fault-finding, which can lead easily to cursing and bemoaning our lot. Such choices are not life-giving. In hard times we must work to "choose life." Each choice of ours strengthens the likelihood of the next choice following it in kind. Choosing "death" makes it more likely that we'll repeat the same choice the next time, unless we consciously choose otherwise.

Even though I find it difficult, loving God, help me to choose life. In all the struggles of my life, let me decide to say and do things that affirm life and cause me to grow, even when it's easier to just be angry and bitter. Make each step I take through my hard times be a step toward you. Then I will always be choosing life.

the**WORD** among us®
The *Spirit* of Catholic Living

This book was published by The Word Among Us. Since 1981, The Word Among Us has been answering the call of the Second Vatican Council to help Catholic laypeople encounter Christ in the Scriptures.

The name of our company comes from the prologue to the Gospel of John and reflects the vision and purpose of all of our publications: to be an instrument of the Spirit, whose desire is to manifest Jesus' presence in and to the children of God. In this way, we hope to contribute to the Church's ongoing mission of proclaiming the gospel to the world so that all people would know the love and mercy of our Lord and grow ever more deeply in love with him.

Our monthly devotional magazine, *The Word Among Us*, features meditations on the daily and Sunday Mass readings, and currently reaches more than one million Catholics in North America and another half million Catholics in one hundred countries around the world. Our book division, The Word Among Us Press, publishes numerous books, Bible studies, and pamphlets that help Catholics grow in their faith.

To learn more about who we are and what we publish, log on to our website at www.wau.org. There you will find a variety of Catholic resources that will help you grow in your faith.

Embrace His Word, Listen to God . . .

wau.org

Made in the USA
Columbia, SC
16 March 2018